Using the Bible

in

Worship

Edited by

Christopher Byworth

Rector of Thetford, Norfolk

GROVE BOOKS

BRAMCOTE NOTTS.

CONTENTS

THE CONTRIBUTORS

Anthony Thiselton is lecturer in Theology in the University of Sheffield and is author of Grove Liturgical Study No. 2 *Language Liturgy and Meaning* (1975).

Christopher Byworth is rector of Thetford, Norfolk, and is joint-author of Grove Booklet on Ministry and Worship No. 5 *A Service of Thanksgiving and Blessing* (1972) and author of No. 8 *Communion, Confirmation and Commitment* (1972).

David Frost is a Professor of English in the University of Newcastle, New South Wales, is a member of the Church of England Liturgical Commission, and is author of Grove Booklet on Ministry and Worship No. 12 *The Language of Series 3* (1973). He is joint-translator and editor of *The Psalms: A New Translation for Worship* (Collins 1977).

John Tiller is vicar of Christ Church, Bedford, and is editor of Grove Booklet on Ministry and Worship No. 23 *A Modern Liturgical Bibliography* (1974).

Ian Bunting is Director of Pastoral Studies at Cranmer Hall, St. John's College, Durham.

[The contributors refer to their other writings in footnotes]

First Impression September 1977

ISSN 0306 0608
ISBN 0 905422 21 X

INTRODUCTION

At the time of writing the Series 3 Communion service has recently received in a widespread questionnaire an 85% vote of general support by the parishes. Yet over these last months it has also encountered a skirmishing attack. There have been recurrent grumbles in *Theology* about the language of the rite.[1] There has been a seminal complaint by a member of the Liturgical Commission itself[2]; and there is the attack by Tom Baker in a book published this July.[3] The point of attack is that the language is drawn broadly and deeply from the language of scripture, using the thought-forms and imagery of scripture with great freedom. It seems to need a donnish dog in a scholarly manger to treat this feature as a *handicap*, when it is proving popular at parish level. Their basic criticism of this biblicism is that it does not reflect the findings of modern theology or biblical research. Christian truth, it is asserted, is now being restated in different terms, and this should be reflected in popular rites. *The Myth of God Incarnate*[4] is not directly liturgical, and therefore not directly in view here; but our conclusions can be seen to apply easily to parts of it, and Anthony Thiselton has added a brief note about it to his essay.[5]

One of our great difficulties is the lack of an obvious alternative vocabulary and imagery, coming from the critics of biblical language. We had to cast around for any constructive alternative that could be taken seriously. It is ironical, and perhaps unfair, that John Macquarrie's was the only one I could find. It seems ironical since Michael Green has rightly cast him among the champions of traditional faith in his *The Truth of God Incarnate*.[6] It is also a little unfair since the book criticized is a work of theology not liturgy. Nevertheless he does propose and work out an alternative language for theology and to me seems to change the content as well as the presentation of traditional Christianity.

It is this sense that large questions are at stake which has determined the shape of the symposium. The restatement of principles over against three specific critics comes first—then there follow two chapters by John Tiller and Ian Bunting exemplifying the use still to be made of the 'ministry of the word' in the liturgy. Between the various authors there is some overlapping, which establishes that there is a common standpoint. Our chief concern has been with principles for writing liturgy.

Having said that, in the light of the earlier remark that 'large questions are at stake' we yet do not claim to have answered all the questions definitively. But we dare to hope that others who enter the field will *prove* us wrong if they wish to take other ground, and also that the 'other ground' of alternative vocabularies and thought forms will be sufficiently clearly laid out for us as to be able to locate and inspect them.

Perhaps Series 3 did not get it so far wrong after all.

Christopher Byworth 2 September 1977

As, e.g. by John Drury in Vol. LXXIX, May 1976, No. 669, pp.130-1.

J. L. Houlden, 'Liturgy and her Companions' in R. C. D. Jasper (ed.) *The Eucharist To-Day: Studies on Series 3* (S.P.C.K., 1974).

T. G. A. Baker, *Questioning Worship* (S.C.M., July 1977).

J. Hick (ed.) *The Myth of God Incarnate* (S.C.M., June 1977).

See p.12 below.

E. M. B. Green (ed.) *The Truth of God Incarnate* (Hodder, August 1977) pp.140-144.

1. MYTH, PARADIGM, AND THE STATUS OF BIBLICAL IMAGERY

by Anthony C. Thiselton

In a recent essay entitled 'Liturgy and her Companions: a Theological Appraisal', J. L. Houlden raises three problems about the use of the Bible in liturgy.[1] Firstly, there is the problem of myth. Does the church of the present, he asks, really wish to articulate its worship in idioms which are often mythological? 'Demythologizing . . . can . . . lead to a restoration of a sense of the living God by removing the opiate of an obsolete story'.[2] Secondly, there is the problem of intelligibility. We must ask not only whether Biblical imagery still retains its former vividness, but also whether it still provides 'intelligible expressions of what is to be said.'[3] Thirdly, we run up against the problem of context. Houlden warns us: 'We hardly safeguard Christian truth merely by uttering its old words out of context and unexplained.'[4]

It is utterly right that these questions should be raised. The present short essay, far from rejecting their relevance, simply seeks to take the discussion a little further. Indeed it is worth noting that these three questions have been raised in a manner which is entirely moderate and restrained and that the writer might well have gone much further in underlining the difficulties to which he refers. For example, he fully recognizes that liturgy is not merely a matter of letting modern man express his own modern attitudes and outlooks. He allows that demythologizing, whether mild or severe, may lead negatively to an impoverishment of imagery. Furthermore he might well have drawn on the kind of arguments about historical disturbance and historical relativism that are put forward by Dennis Nineham in his lecture *New Testament Interpretation in an Historical Age* (1976) and his full-scale book *The Use and Abuse of the Bible* (1976). The problem of context, as cited by Houlden, becomes still more difficult when it is viewed within this kind of framework. Thus C. F. Evans claims that in this respect one of the most serious difficulties about using the Bible today is 'the problem of . . . how what is intelligible in its original context can be taken over and used apart from that context *without in the process altering its meaning'*.[5]

We may begin with the problem of myth. It is important to note that the argument about myth rests not on one issue, but on two. The argument may be said to run as follows. (1) Major premise: the Bible uses mythological language. (2) Minor premise: mythological language cannot be used with complete propriety by modern man. (3) Conclusion: therefore modern

---

[1] R. C. D. Jasper (ed.) *The Eucharist Today: Studies on Series 3* (S.P.C.K. London, 1974) pp.168-76.

[2] *Ibid.* p.172. For reference to *The Myth of God Incarnate* see p.12 below.

[3] *Ibid.* p.173.

[4] *Ibid.* p.174.

[5] C. F. Evans in *Christian Believing. A Report by the Doctrine Commission of the Church of England* (S.P.C.K. London, 1976) p.49.

4

man cannot use certain parts of the Bible (e.g. in liturgy) with propriety. Admittedly in practice the argument would not be expressed so baldly; but it does usually rest on taking two distinct steps. Firstly, it rests on an assumption about the nature of the language of the Bible; and secondly, it rests on an assumption about modern man.

A logical syllogism stands up if the link-term of the argument retains consistently the same meaning, but not if that term is used ambiguously. (The classic example of such ambiguity in a theological argument is the cosmological argument for the existence of God. It is generally agreed that the problem here is that whilst every event normally has a caused cause, the universe is said to have an uncaused cause. In other words, 'cause' takes on an added meaning). In the case of the argument about myth, it is usually the word 'myth' that causes the problem. If myth is defined sufficiently *broadly,* almost everyone will agree that the Bible uses mythological language. But the minor premise that suggests that myth is inappropriate for modern man presupposes a *narrower and more specific* understanding of myth. Indeed it is an understanding of myth which, if used in the major premise that the Bible uses mythological language, would lead to the rejection of this premise on the part of many scholars.

Let us now look more closely at this pivotal question of how myth is defined, and whether it can be defined consistently in both stages of the argument. To begin with, we may set aside as entirely irrelevant the popular modern notion of myth as that which is necessarily false. In all serious discussion, as John Knox puts it, 'the term really designates a kind of speech, a category of discourse, and is neutral as regards the question of truth. A myth can be false or true'.[1] Indeed even this standpoint is possible only *outside* the community for which the myth functions as myth. *Within* the language-community concerned, myth has the status of believed truth. More positively, there are perhaps three features which virtually all scholars (whether of anthropology, folk-lore, literature, or religion) would attribute to myth. (1) In the setting of their own community, myths possess, or at least once possessed, the status of believed truth. (2) Myths emerge from within the life of a community, answering to some significant feature of its common belief or culture. (3) Myths use narrative form, depicting events, and never use the form of abstract generalization. Usually, myths tell stories about divine beings, in contrast to legends which tell tales about human heroes.

These three characteristics, however, remain so broad and unspecific that they really tell us very little that relates to our present problems. Yet as soon as we try to define myth more specifically, it begins to become apparent that from this point onwards the term is no longer used consistently by various groups of scholars. For example, O. Eissfeldt contends that 'a real myth presupposes at least two gods'.[2] On this view, myth would be unacceptable to modern man, but is hardly a major feature of Biblical language. On the other hand Emil Brunner and John Knox define myth in a way which wholly accords with Biblical monotheism. But they use the term so positively and favourably that they also explicitly contend that

John Knox, *Myth and Truth* (Carey Kingsgate Press, London, 1966) p.18.
O. Eissfeldt, *The Old Testament. An Introduction* (Blackwell, Oxford, 1965) p.35.

modern man needs myth.[1] Knox insists that Christological myths 'are an expression of the *Church's* existence', designating 'the distinctive inner being of a particular historical community'. They convey 'the concrete meaning of Christ himself, both remembered and present, which is the very breath of the Church's existence'.[2] If either of these two approaches to myth were adapted consistently, we should then meet two alternative forms of argument. On the basis of Eissfeldt's approach, the argument would run: myth is inappropriate to modern man, but there is no myth in the New Testament. On the basis of Knox's approach, the argcment would run: there is myth in the New Testament, but modern man cannot dispense with such myth.

By now the reader may have become impatient. Have we not made everything too easy by over-simplifying and polarizing the argument? Is there not more to the matter than this? Certainly there is. But even wher allowance is made for the most sophisticated discussion of myth, the shape of the problem remains that which has been crudely outlined. In the space of a few pages we cannot even begin to set out the complex issues which major discussions of myth lay before us. Perhaps the best that we can do is to outline the issues further with reference to two standard discussions in German theology. The first is the classic survey undertaken by G Hartlich and W. Sachs under the title *Der Ursprung des Mythosbegriffes in der modernen Bibelwissenschaft,* published in 1952. The second is the modern discussion of Rudolf Bultmann's proposals about demythologizing which by now have settled into fairly well-worn grooves. I am encouraged to think that the discussion has now entered this phase not least on the basis of oral comments made to me to this effect by Hans-Werner Bartsch the editor of the six volumes and additional supplements entitled *Kerygma und Mythos,* which report much of this discussion.

I follow those modern writers (including especially Roger A. Johnson who draw a careful distinction between three main views of myth which are found both in German theology in general and in Bultmann in particular. Firstly, there is the *religionsgeschichtliche* formulation of myth found i Richard Reitzenstein, Wilhelm Bousset, and other writers of the history-of religions school. Myth is here viewed in terms of a particular soteriologica narrative-structure, according to which a heavenly redeemer, primal mar or divine hero, descends from heaven and intervenes in earthly affairs Myth takes the form of a cosmic drama, which is recited in the context o the cult. Such theories, especially as they occur in Reitzenstein, hav undergone decisive criticism, both in themselves and in terms of the applicability to the New Testament, at the hands of Carsten Colpe.[4] In th sense specified by *this* definition of myth, it is highly doubtful that we ca

---

[1] E. Brunner, *The Mediator* (Lutterworth, London, 1934) pp.377-96; and J. Knox, *o cot.,* pp.18-50 *et passim.*

[2] J. Knox, *op. cit.* p.49.

[3] Roger A. Johnson, *The Origins of Demythologizing. Philosophy and Historiography the Theology of Rudolf Bultmann* (Brill, Leiden, 1974).

[4] Carsten Colpe, *Die religionsgeschichtliche Schule. Darstellung und Kritik ihre Bildes vom gnostischen Erlosermythus* (Vandenhoek and Ruprecht, Gottinge 1961).

legitimately claim that much of the language of the New Testament is mythological. Far from establishing that the New Testament draws on this pattern of mythology, many writers allow that the basic gnostic, Mandean and hellenistic-religious sources cited for such myths actually post-date New Testament Christianity. Here, then, is a view of myth which would be inappropriate for the use of the modern Christian community, but at the same time is unlikely to be present in the New Testament. As Johnson clearly shows, even Bultmann himself, who drew on this view of myth during the years 1920-33, tended to move away from it in subsequent years in favour of a different understanding of myth suggested by the work of Hans Jonas.[1]

Secondly, there is the so-called Enlightenment view of myth. Here we meet the very essence of the outlook that myth is necessarily primitive and incompatible with life in the modern age of science. Modern man, it is claimed, works by observation, abstraction, testing, and rigorous logic. By this means he arrives at objective knowledge. But primitive man, it is urged, did not possess the capacity for such abstract reasoning. His thinking was naive, pre-rational, pre-critical, and pre-logical. In the view of the philosophers and theologians of the Enlightenment, this pre-critical mode of thinking was what characterized myth. It is *necessarily* bound up with a primitive world-view. Thus, for example, an ignorance of medicine and psychiatry led men to ascribe illness to demons and sudden cures to the miraculous intervention of the Spirit of God. This view of myth came to expression in the writings of Bernard Fontanelle in 1724. Hartlich and Sachs show how it decisively influenced the approaches to the Biblical writings of R. Lowth in the eighteenth century, and C. G. Heyne in the nineteenth century, leading to J. G. Eichorn's claims about the Old Testament and D. F. Strauss's claims about the New Testament.[2] The philosopher Ernst Cassirer, who was influenced in the Neo-Kantian intellectual circles in which Bultmann moved, was one of the main exponents of this view. According to the mythical outlook, Cassirer writes, 'Subjective excitement becomes objectified, and confronts the mind as a god or a demon'.[3] It is in this context that we are to understand Bultmann's remarks about myth and modern man when he asserts, 'It is impossible to use electric light and the miracles, and to avail ourselves of modern medical and surgical discoveries, and at the same time to believe in the New Testament world of spirits and miracles.'[4]

It is open to question, however, whether New Testament allusions to the supernatural world rest on considerations cited by the philosophers and theologians of the Enlightenment. A belief in the supernatural activity of God within the world does not depend on uncritical thinking or scientific ignorance. On the basis of such a view we should certainly not expect to find philosophers and scientists today who can whole-heartedly endorse belief in supernatural realities. Indeed, in practice it has been claimed that

R. A. Johnson, *op. cit.*, pp.103-126 and 207-31.
Christian Hartlich and Walter Sachs, *Der Ursprung des Mythosbegriffes in der modernen Bibelwissenschaft* (Mohr, Tubingen, 1952) pp.6-19, 87-90, and 148-64.
Ernst Cassirer, *Language and Myth* (Harper, New York, 1946) p.33.
R. Bultmann, 'The New Testament and Mythology' in H.-W. Bartsch (ed.) *Kerygma and Myth* I (S.P.C.K. London, 1964) pp.4-5.

it is the Enlightenment view of science (shared by Bultmann) which is old-fashioned. In spite of claims to the contrary by S. M. Ogden and W. Schmithals, there is much justice in J. Macquarrie's comment that 'we perceive in Bultmann's thought . . . the hangover of a somewhat old-fashioned liberal modernism. He is still obsessed with the pseudo-scientific view of a closed universe that was popular half a century ago'.[1] More positively, the issue is admirably expressed by Wolfhart Pannenberg. He writes, 'The acceptance of divine intervention in the course of events . . . is fundamental to *every religious* understanding of the world, including one which is not mythical.'[2] Thus Pannenberg concludes that neither eschatology nor even the belief in demons as such is specifically mythological.[3]

We move on, then, to the third main conception of myth which is found in the German theological discussion. Johnson describes this as the existentialist formulation of myth, although this is only one of several possible ways of identifying it. It rests on a fundamental distinction between the logic of bare description and the logic of self-involvement. In Bultmann's thought it is closely bound up with the problem of objectification, in accordance with the legacy of Neo-Kantian philosophy. Bultmann writes, 'The real purpose of myth is not to present an objective picture of the world as it is *(ein objektives Weltbild)* but to express *man's understanding of himself* in the world in which he lives. Myth should be interpreted not cosmologically but . . . existentially.'[4] Myth needs to be interpreted, Bultmann argues, because the actual form of mythological language in the New Testament obscures its intended function. It looks as if it is describing an objective state of affairs; but in reality it serves to call man himself to take up certain responses and attitudes. For example, 'God will judge the world at the last day' takes the form of a descriptive assertion about a future event. But its intention, it is agreed, is really to call men to accept responsibility for their conduct. What look like statements about Christological achievements or an eschatological programme are in reality intended as self-involving utterances.

We do not deny that there is a measure of truth in this account of certain New Testament utterances. The statement that God will judge the world is not *simply* a bare statement. What remains doubtful, however, is whether utterances of this kind can be interpreted existentially *exhaustively and without remainder.* The statement that God will judge the world draws its very self-involving character from the fact that it is no mere religious idea, no mere bluff, but actually makes an assertion about a future certainty. Admittedly Bultmann himself argues that the New Testament, on its own terms, demands demythologizing of this kind. He insists 'to demythologize is to reject not scripture . . . but the world-view of scripture, which is the world-view of a past epoch'. Thereby the interpreter will 'eliminate a false

1 J. Macquarrie, *An Existentialist Theology* (S.C.M. London 1955 rp. Pelican, 1973 p.158. For a contrary view, cf. S. M. Ogden, *Christ without Myth* (Collins, London 1962) 38-9.
2 W. Pannenberg, 'Myth in Biblical and Christian Tradition' in *Basic Questions in Theology* III (S.C.M. London, 1973) p.14.
3 *Ibid.* pp.67 and 68.
4 R. Bultmann, *loc. cit.* I, p.10 (German, I, p.23).

stumbling-block and bring into sharp focus the real stumbling-block the word of the cross.'[1] We sympathize with Bultmann's intention. Indeed if 'demythologizing' meant only bringing out more clearly the self-involving character of New Testament language, we should endorse Bultmann's programme. In practice, however, it means more than this. Bultmann himself not only concedes, but also insists, that in the area of Christology the issue finds decisive expression in the question of whether Christological language says anything genuinely descriptive about Christ, or whether it only expresses what Christ is *for me.* This comes out clearly in his well-known essay of 1951 on the Christological Confession of the World Council of Churches.[2] Commenting on the question 'Does Christ help me because he is God's Son, or is he the Son of God because he helps me?', Bultmann opts firmly for the latter alternative.

It is false, however, to draw such a sharp distinction between the language of fact and the language of value. Bultmann draws this distinction because, like Wittgenstein in the *Tractatus,* he is grappling with the legacy of Neo-Kantian philosophy. But the English-speaking world has never accepted such a radical dualism in the first place, and even on the Continent it has been subjected to decisive criticism at the hands of such theologians as Heinrich Ott and Wofhart Pannenberg. I have developed this point in another study which is at present awaiting publication.[3] Meanwhile, we may take up an analogy suggested by Ian Henderson. There are two kinds of interpretation, he suggests. One may be compared to the translation of a code. Once we have the translation, the original may be dispensed with. The other is like a commentary on a masterpiece. The commentary may serve to highlight certain points, and to guard against misunderstandings; but we return again and again to the original itself, which is certainly not dispensable. We suggest that a recognition of the self-involving character of New Testament language is incompatible with the first type of interpretation, but is fully congruent with the second.

It would be possible at this point to show that many writers, including Eliade, Jaspers, Jung, and Berdyaev, insist upon the value of myth for modern man. But this would raise further problems about the different senses in which the term 'myth' is used. We may conclude this stage of the discussion by saying that if by 'myth' we mean self-involving narrative, there is certainly no need to dispense with Biblical language, provided that it is indeed understood to be self-involving. But usually liturgy brings out this very aspect of the language. It is in the context of doctrinal statement that language, for example about Christ's lordship or ascension may be all too easily reduced to mean 'statement'. In liturgy such truths are more usually not 'stated', but 'acclaimed' or 'celebrated'. On the other hand, when the term 'myth' is used in its Enlightenment sense to designate pre-critical thinking, it is dubious to what extent this approach is relevant to questions about the New Testament. Admittedly very much more can be said on this

R. Bultmann, *Jesus Christ and Mythology* (S.C.M. ,London, 1960) pp.35-6.

R. Bultmann, *Essays Philosophical and Theological* (ET, S.C.M. London, 1955) pp.273-90; *Glauben und Verstehen* (Mohr, Tubingen, 1964) II, pp.245-61.

A. C. Thiselton, *New Testament Hermeneutics and Philosophical Description* (Sheffield Ph.D. thesis, 1977). Approx. 600pp.

subject, from more than one side, and I have discussed these questions more fully elsewhere.[1] However, before we conclude these few short comments, we must also glance briefly at the other two issues raised in the essay by Houlden to which we have referred.

Like myth, the Bible concerns not only ideas but also events. Moreover there is something unique and irreplaceable about the foundation-events of the Christian community, that the Bible narrates. These two points bear closely on the problem of *meaning*. The problem of communicating meaning in religious language is certainly not solved by seeking to re-label the traditional Christian vocabulary. Such a move, as Gerhard Ebeling rightly insists, is merely superficial. To quote Ebeling himself, 'the problem lies too deep to be tackled by the mere borrowing of words . . . [it] concerns not simply words, but "the word".'[2] In more than three separate studies I have urged that the key to the problem of the meaning of language in religion lies in the relation between language and life, especially along the lines suggested by the philosopher Ludwig Wittgenstein in his later writings.[3] In these studies I have tried to argue that the Biblical writings set forth a tradition of language-uses which can be correlated with patterns of events and human behaviour in such a way as to provide the basis for solving the problem of meaning in language used by the Christian community.

It is impossible to summarize the arguments of these studies in only two or three pages. However, we may indicate briefly the direction of the approach. Firstly, we endorse Wittgenstein's verdict that the problem of meaning cannot be solved by appeal to ostensive definition and theories of reference. One of his key concepts is that of the 'language-game'. Wittgenstein writes, 'The term language-*game*' is meant to bring into prominence the fact that the speaking of language is part of an activity, or of a form of life *(Lebensform).'*[4] In his *Zettel* he asserts 'Only in the stream of thought and life do words have meaning'.[5] Secondly, this has significance for questions about communication and learning. 'One learns the game by watching how others play'.[6] The problem of learning to understand the game, is *not* solved merely by re-labelling the positions or roles of all the players in a more 'modern' way. It is solved by watching the inter-relation between language and human behaviour. Thirdly, a tradition must be built up, whereby *regularities* may be observed on the basis of which given language-users and given situations may be correlated with each

---

[1] *Op. cit.* 357-420; and 'Myth, Mythology' in the *Zondervan Encyclopedia of the Bible* (Zondervan, Grand Rapids, Mich., U.S.A., 1975) IV, pp.333-43.

[2] G. Ebeling, *The Nature of Faith* (ET, Collins, Glasgow, 1961) 15; cf. *Introduction to a Theological Theory of Language* (ET, Collins, Glasgow, 1973) pp.91-128.

[3] A. C. Thiselton, *Language, Liturgy, and Meaning* (Grove Liturgical Studies 2, Nottingham, 1975); 'Language and Meaning in Religion' in C. Brown (ed.) *New International Dictionary of New Testament Theology* III (Paternoster, Exeter, 1977 forthcoming) and *New Testament Hermeneutics and Philosophical Description* pp.518-606.

[4] L. Wittgenstein, *Philosophical Investigations* (Blackwell, Oxford, 2 1958) sect. 23.

[5] L. Wittgenstein, *Zettel* (Blackwell, Oxford, 1967) sect. 173.

[6] L. Wittgenstein, *Philosophical Investigations* sect. 54.

other. For example, I may discern certain elements of continuity between various situations portrayed in the Israelite narratives and uses of such terms as 'save' or 'redeem' in Biblical language. Such situations throw up 'public' criteria of meaning; whereas 'private' language (i.e. one which is unrelated in any way to observable events or behaviour) would be necessarily unteachable. Fourthly, in addition to providing public criteria of meaning in the context of an ongoing tradition, Biblical language is also *paradigmatic* for later Christian language-uses. For it concerns the foundation events which give the Christian community its very identity.

The concept of the paradigm case is a familiar one in linguistic philosophy, and occurs at least in effect in the writings of G. E. Moore. A frequent example is that which concerns the use of the word 'solid'. Physicists sometimes tell us that such things as marble tables or oak beams are not really 'solid', since scientifically they consist of atoms moving through space. But this is simply to ask us to re-define what we mean by 'solid'. 'Solid' derives its very currency from its application to things like marble slabs and oak beams. There are paradigm-cases of the meaning of the word. Wittgenstein considers attempts to re-define certain rock-bottom meanings, and drily remarks 'I must not saw off the branch on which I am sitting'. The Biblical writings, we maintain, provide paradigm-cases of meanings in the Christian vocabulary. To jettison the classic concepts of the Biblical writings would be, in terms of the problem of meaning, to 'saw off the branch on which I am sitting'. To be sure these concepts may be extended and interpreted; but to dispense with them would be to lose hold of that which gives the Christian community its very identity. Far from solving the problem of meaning, it would only introduce unnecessary confusion. It would take away the very tradition on the basis of which Christian language-uses acquire intelligibility. For it would remove language from the 'life' that first gave it breath, and make the problem of *identity* and *continuity* insoluble.

J. L. Houlden's third point concerns the use of Biblical imagery when it is taken out of context. We have great sympathy with this criticism, and must allow that it is sometimes valid. Wittgenstein's work suggests that confusions do indeed arise when language is used outside its own proper language-game: 'The language-game in which they are to be applied is missing'.[1] But Biblical imagery cannot for this reason be excluded from liturgy as a matter of universal *principle.* What is required is that those who compose the liturgy should exercise all possible care in assessing whether the contexts of such imagery are *in practice* such as to undermine the meaning which it has in its own language-game.

An awesome warning against irresponsible use of Biblical imagery occurs in the early gnostic writings. A study of this tragic transformation of semantic values is offered by Samuel Laeuchli.[2] Words like *'gnosis', 'aeon',* and *'pleroma'* are taken out of the text of the New Testament itself, and are used in contexts which force totally new meanings upon them. Laeuchli rightly speaks of 'a tension between the meaning in its original frame and

Ibid. sect. 96.

S. Laeuchli, *The Language of Faith. An Introduction to the Semantic Dilemma of the Early Church* (Epworth Press, London, 1965).

the new frame into which it is inserted . . . Phrases stand in another light'.[1] There is a 'reversal of meaning of seemingly biblical terms'.[2] Laeuchli concludes, ' "Canonical language" demands . . . comprehension of the whole—"Canonical language" is only possible in a chain of biblical terminology, never in a catchword or in a set phrase, but in the relation of biblical concepts to each other'.[3]

If this warning is valid, and I believe that it is, the consequence is clear. Any move to include *less* Biblical imagery in liturgy will be counter-productive, unless we abandon *all* Biblical imagery. As it is, provided that the liturgy as a whole is structured in a way that reflects the paradigmatic language of the Bible, even relatively allusive stretches of Biblical imagery may in principle function with positive effect. Roland Bartel makes this point about allusions to the Bible in literature. He writes, 'A successful allusion operates like a metaphor. It is, in fact, an implied comparison in that it invites the reader to use his knowledge of the Bible to interpret the material before him. When Thoreau concludes one of his paragraphs in "Spring" (in *Walden*) with the words . . . "O Death, where was thy sting? O Grave, where was thy victory?" we realize what the melting of the ice and the greening of the vegetation meant to him'.[4] In other words, we have now moved from myth, through paradigm, to conceptual metaphor or *model.*

Even here, once again, we may cite Wittgenstein's later work in order to underline the importance of such uses of images. For Wittgenstein insists that pictures can dictate to us a whole way of seeing a problem, or even of seeing life. Yet he also warns us that such pictures may be variously interpreted. If those who write liturgies draw on Biblical imagery, they are engaging both the imagination and vision of the worshipper, as well as his intellect, in ways which may exercise great power on his attitudes.

The moral to be drawn is that such powerful forces should be used only with great caution and care; that liturgists should draw on Biblical imagery only when they can do so sensitively and responsibly with full awareness of the issues involved. But it certainly does not suggest that Biblical imagery should be abandoned. Indeed the very reverse is the case.

APPENDED NOTE

The book *The Myth of God Incarnate,* edited by John Hick (1977) was published after the completion of this essay (although the essay on myth by Professor Maurice Wiles makes use of previously-published material). Wiles sets out some of the problems that are raised by varied uses of the term 'myth' in theology. But his awareness of the problem does little to alleviate the difficulties caused by the varied ways in which it is used within the covers of this one volume. Michael Goulder and Frances Young use the term to refer to specific myths in the ancient Graeco-Roman world, and Stephen Neill has admirably criticized the applicability of myth in this sense to New Testament Christology (in Michael Green (ed.) *The Truth of God Incarnate,* 1977, pp.60-66). But Frances Young also uses the term broadly to mean indirect or analogical discourse which cannot be expressed in scientific or univocal language. She even uses the phrase 'anthropo-morphic or "mythological" language' (p.35). The words of caution offered by Wiles are effectively ignored in the rest of the book.

[1] *Op. cit.* p.19.
[2] *Ibid.* p.43.
[3] *Ibid.* p.91.
[4] R. Bartel (ed.) *Biblical Images in Literature* (Abingdon, New York 1975) p.14.

2. CAN WE RE-WRITE THEOLOGY IN NON-BIBLICAL TERMS?
An examination of John Macquarrie's exploration of existential-ontological languages
by Christopher Byworth

Well, the title, and even more the sub-title, should have put you off! The point of this essay is to look at the rationale and assess the success of a notable attempt to rewirte theology in a 'modern', rather than a 'biblical', terminology. Its relevance to this liturgical study is that it is precisely this that Leslie Houlden[1] and Tom Baker[2] urge us to do in liturgy, or at least to enshrine the findings of modern theology in our modern liturgies and to refrain from excessive biblicism and biblical imagery. The examination is taken from John Macquarrie's *Principles of Christian Theology* (S.C.M., 1966) which is a profound and fresh restatement of much basic Christian doctrine in what he calls 'existential-ontological language'. Indeed it is only an analysis of two chapters of that book, chapters six and eight, though illustrations are drawn from other parts of it as well.

But is this process fair? Is it fair to assume that it is this type of language that Leslie Houlden or Tom Baker is recommending for our new liturgies? We cannot be certain (for their own alternatives do not appear), but presumably it is something along these lines, and certainly using these insights. It is clear that they wish to reject traditional, biblical imagery, and that is Macquarrie's starting-point. Above all, Macquarrie analyses what he is doing in providing this new language and tells you why; and thus enables us to study both the process and the reasons, to see what we can learn from them, and to discern where we want to question them.

First, I shall look through Macquarrie's eyes at the whole problem of using religious language to communicate truth about God today. Then, I shall follow him actually doing theology and look at his methodology. Thirdly, I shall look at his reasons for valuing the existential-ontological language as the most adequate expression of theology today. After this, I will conclude by seeing what lessons we can learn from him and the places where we should question his presuppositions, approach and findings.

The problems of communicating

The problems of communicating are several. First it is clear that words do not always express what we mean, though they are far more likely to do so when we talk to someone who has had similar experiences and is sympathetic. Thus we find that religious language communicates most effectively within the community of believers. This, of course, raises the question of how biblical language, drawn as it is from the religious experience of cultures and ages far removed from our own, can communicate with us today, even if we have had religious experiences. It is to this point that Anthony Thistelton's essay speaks in particular. However, a second problem arises when we examine the types of language used in religious discourse. Macquarrie finds five types of religious language: myth, analogy, history, that is the recording of events interpreted as divine acts,

[1] R. C. D. Jasper (ed.) *The Eucharist Today, Studies on Series 3* (S.P.C.K. London, 1974) pp.168-176.
[2] T. G. A. Baker *Questioning Worship* S.C.M. 1977.

dogma such as credal statements, and 'practical' language such as ethical instruction and liturgy. On Bultmann's use of demythologizing, Macquarrie makes the important point that to take all elements of myth as descriptive only of our inner life, misses their transcendent reference. The often 'talk' ontologically as well, though only by analogy of course. The key point about all this language, and indeed any religious language, is that it can only be symbolic. By this Macquarrie seems to mean 'true by analogy'. To choose an oft-taken example, God is spoken of as Father, and our concept of fatherhood derives from that of human fatherhood. Thus, when it is used of God it must be denied as well as asserted, since the reality of God's fatherhood cannot be contained within our human concept.

So far Macquarrie has made two important points. First that the distance between our life situation and thought-forms and those many different different ones of the Bible is such as to make effective communication very hard. Second, he says that all religious language is perforce symbolic or analogous, and cannot be a fully satisfactory expression of the truth about God. A symbol is 'anything which is presented to the mind as standing for something else'. Thus the word 'light' when referred to Christ is symbolic. The most adequate symbols are not the merely conventional ones, such as the Union Jack for the United Kingdom, but ones where there is an intrinsic connection, such as Christ as the light. Then a new understanding is achieved. Best of all for theology are those symbols which convey meaning to the widest possible audience. This is to be an important reason for Macquarrie choosing his 'existential-ontological' language in which to recast theology.

Finally, Macquarrie looks at the factors involved in religious verbal communication. He finds three. First there is the person speaking. His words express his hidden thought or experience as well as his commitment to them. Next there are the words spoken. These refer ultimately to Being, Macquarrie's term for God. But, since these words were originally used to describe 'beings' (that is, the things and experiences of ordinary human existence), when they are used of Being, the words have to be 'stretched' since they are being used by analogy. Lastly there is the person spoken to. He shares the thought or experience of the speaker, only if he is in the same frame of mind, that is, only if he has the same world view. It is for precisely this reason that the old religious myths do not communicate today, but need translating, claims Macquarrie.

Macquarrie's Methodology
How then does one write or communicate theology today? Macquarrie recommends a three-stage process, and casts his book in this shape. First, there must be philosophical theology which uses the method of description. By this Macquarrie is referring to describing what man experiences of himself and the world. He uses Husserl's phenomenology to discover what these experiences mean to people. Thus the key to man is that he alone can have a relationship with himself, as can be seen in such remarks as 'I hate myself for doing that.' Next he looks at the 'polarities' of life. I live in community, and yet my inner self is intensely private, lonely and isolated. There is an immense range of choices open to me, and yet I am not totally free, but limited by my particular personality and situation. I am

rational and yet the irrational drives within me are such that I do not always understand even my own motives. I feel responsible for my own actions and yet am so often impotent to do and be what I feel I ought to do and be. Death would seem to be the final absurdity and yet we go on wanting to live, which testifies to the fact that we believe that we can make sense of existence.

Macquarrie sees man's dilemma as deeply serious, but believes nevertheless that true selfhood (or authentic existence, as he sometimes calls it) is possible. Authentic existence is achieved in man's moment-by-moment decisions. These should be based both on the acceptance of our past and on the commitment to the future. By the latter he means the deliberate aligning and subordinating of all our possibilities to one future master possibility. This commitment to a wider being leads him into an analysis of man in terms of being, and a discussion on the possibility of revelation, that is an unveiling to our experience, where the initiative lies with the one who is becoming known. In R. Otto's words it is an experience of a mysterium tremendum et fascinans.' It is a numinous experience before which one is both awe-struck, almost terrified, and yet to which one is irresistibly drawn. This naturally leads into an examination of God as holy Being or rather a letting-be 'a kind of energy that permits other things to be' rather than a being. Macquarrie's phrase is 'the incomparable that lets be and that is present and manifests itself through the beings.'

The descriptive stage is now over. It has started not with preconceived ideas, but with the phenomenon of the human situation; and it has clarified key terms such as man, sin and being. All is now ready for the second stage, symbolic theology. By this Macquarrie means the main Christian doctrines of the Trinity, Creation, Evil, the Person and Work of Christ, the Spirit and the Last Things. These are all symbols that is, inadequate word pictures, and Macquarrie seeks to recast (and remould?) them in his new existential-ontological language framework. Finally in applied theology, Macquarrie looks at the Church, the Ministry, the Word and Sacraments, Worship and Prayer and Christianity in the world.

Macquarrie's Existential-Ontological language

The crucial point, for the purpose of this essay, is to look at Macquarrie's reasons for making the 'translation' of theology into an existential-ontological language. He claims first that such a translation is possible because of the analogy that exists between Being and beings. This analogy is available simply because Being is present in beings. Because of this, all beings are potential symbols of Being. However, some of these beings, such as the Cross and Fatherhood, have been 'given' to us by Being in an historical revelation, and so they more adequately 'light-up' Being.

Man is himself the highest symbol, for his love points most adequately towards that letting-be which is the very essence of Being. This point is taken up in Macquarrie's picture of Christ as the 'focus of Being'. He then looks more precisely at how symbols, such as the Fatherhood or goodness of God, can illuminate Being. This happens because we have a similar existential response, for instance of awe or loyalty, aroused in us by Being as we do by some beings. For example we can call Being 'good', this word being a symbol, because our feelings or existential response to Being is the same as our response to goodness. Then there is also a similarity, not just in emotional response, but in relationship. For instance the psalmist writes in Psalm 103.13 'as a father pities his children so the Lord pities those who fear him.' Three of the four items in this parallel are known to us in experience, that is father, children and us; and from the relationship between the first pair of beings we can express the relationship between ourselves and Being or 'the Lord'.

However the translation of theology into an existential-onotological language is not a mere academic possibility, it is in fact the best language for Christianity for today. Macquarrie gives three reasons for this claim. First, this existential-ontological language speaks to the widest audience today, for it describes man's universal experience. Thus its impact is not limited to a westernized Christian audience, as (he implies), the traditional language is. Second, he claims that the Christian symbols are lit up by such language and the existential-ontological language itself is then given a deeper reality by these symbols. Here Macquarrie seems to be referring to what is sometimes known as the hermeneutical circle. He gives an example from the emotion of love. From human experience one already knows something of love, and this enables one to enter into a love poem from a very different culture or language. But having entered into it one's own understanding of love has itself been lit up or deepened, and the circle is complete. Similarly Macquarrie believes that the existential ontological language of human experience will help one to understand the traditional Christian symbols which arise from the thought-forms of a different age, and having understood it, these Christian symbols will then profoundly deepen one's understanding of our human experiences, cast as they are in this existential-ontological language.

The lessons to be learnt

Many of the points Macquarrie has made about the need for an alternative language are profound and challenging, and are remarkably similar to Leslie Houlden's and Tom Baker's criticism of the 'biblicism' of the Series 3 services in England.

First and foremost, here is an actual attempt to recast theology in what is today's most influential philosophy, existentialism. Indeed a whole range of modern insights has been brought to bear, the most obvious of which are Husserl's phenomenology, Heidegger's existentialism and the procedure of Linguistic Analysis. There is undoubtedly a real problem, or rather group of problems, in understanding and finding relevant for ourselves both the images so often used in the Bible and the traditional formulations of Christian doctrine, such as the Chalcedonian definition, which draw on Aristotelian categories of thought, and whose terminology in English such as 'substance', 'person', 'being', no longer means to us now what the words originally meant in Greek. Too many conservative theologians seem to delight in simply destroying modern reformulations. This is understandable since so often the latter seem to 'throw out the baby with the bath water'. Sadly though, conservatives often have little or nothing to offer in its place to meet a real need. At least Macquarrie is trying to meet a serious problem, and, in my view, has done so with considerably more success than many other modern theologians.

Then Macquarrie has also wrestled with several of the modern objections to traditional Christianity, for instance the doctrine of creation, the findings of biblical scholarship, the openness to other religions, and the attempt to start from a position that does not presuppose Christian belief. Here, though, I would argue that significant areas of Christian truth have been endangered, and that some of modern man's 'problems' with Christian belief are not really problems or hindrances to faith to most people today.

Thirdly, and this is a point of immense significance, Macquarrie is not prepared to jettison ontology ,as for instance Bultmann seems prepared to do with his demythologizing. He states the transcendence of God and the reality of Christ's divinity. God is not simply and only 'the depth of our being'. Indeed when he writes about revelation, echoes of Barth can be clearly heard.

Fourthly, much of what he writes on language, analogy and symbol is profound and helpful, and seems to have been drawn from the findings of the 'New Hermeneutic'.

Finally, and this is important, it is far from certain that in Macquarrie's own case, he would want to write liturgy the same way he writes theology. The mind gently boggles at the idea of prayers praising the Focus of Being. It is precisely at this point that Houlden and Baker's plea for the incorporating of modern theological insights seems most impractical. It is hard to see how Macquarrie's profound insights could easily be incorporated into the language of the liturgy.

The questions that are raised
The plea to reinterpret the Christian faith for today, so admirable in itself, has when it is attempted, often led to a radical change, or rather several different sets of changes, to the actual beliefs of traditional Christianity. J. B. Phillips wrote his *Ring of Truth* partly in angry reaction to a then recent restatement of theology which had driven a retired clergyman to take his life. In his foreword he writes 'I am not concerned to distort or dilute the Christian faith so that modern undergraduates, for example, can accept it without a murmur . . . let the modern world conform to him (Jesus Christ) and never let us dare to try to make him fit into our clever-clever modern world. I am not anti-intellectual . . . But I say quite bluntly that some of the intellectuals (by no means all, thank God!) who write so cleverly and devastatingly about the Christian faith appear to have no personal knowledge of the living God. For they lack awe, they lack humility, and they lack the responsibility which every Christian owes to his weaker brother. They make sure that they are never made "fools for Christ's sake", however many people's faith they may undermine.'

Now I do not believe that Phillips' strictures can simply be applied to John Macquarrie's book, but there does seem to have been significant alterations to some traditional beliefs and all presumably in the name of modern man. I mention just some of these. Despite remarks about God's transcendence, the emphasis looks suspiciously like a new form of panentheism, which is the belief that everything exists in God. How would Macquarrie answer the question 'If the world of beings ceased to exist, would Being still exist?', one wonders. Again the distinctiveness of Christ as the only way to God, the role of the Bible as authoritative for the believer's and the church's life, the view of sin as deliberate disobedience to the known will of God, all seem to be called in question.

So it may be doubted if it is Christianity, as it has been traditionally understood, that Macquarrie is seeking to communicate. But how effective has he been in actually helping modern man to faith? The criteria for such a pragmatic test are hard to come by. But I wonder if it is not written more for the modern puzzled Christian than the outsider. I have the gravest doubts whether more than a few hundred non-Christians have read th book, and whether more than that number, Christian, or non-Christian, would understand it. It was a set text for the London University Bachelor of Divinity degree for some time, and was certainly not easily understood by the students I taught, even when they made a detailed study of it.

Thirdly, it is worth mentioning in the whole debate over communicating the Christian faith, that both biblical teaching and pastoral experience endorse the truth that 'the unspiritual man does not receive the gifts of the Spirit of God, for they are folly to him, and he is not able to understand them because they are spiritually discerned' (1 Cor. 2.14—see also Mk. 4.11-13 Jh. 16.7-11, 2 Cor. 4.4). I do not make this point because I wish in any way to underestimate the vital and difficult role of effective communication today or to sidestep much hard thinking and imagination by such an appeal, but because so often it neither gets a mention nor seems to come into the consideration of those, including Macquarrie perhaps, who write on this theme.

Finally, I doubt very much if, on the whole, the biblical imagery and many of the traditional formulations of Christian truth are harder to understand and so communicate less well that Macquarrie's modern formulation. Of course any language about God is inadequate to the truth. But a belief in the incarnation, not to mention a belief that God speaks through the scriptures, implies that God has cut himself down to our size in order to communicate with us. This cutting down is not of course the whole truth, but there is no reason why it should not be true in so far as it goes. If God did choose to reveal himself in particular historic acts and their God-given interpretation, then presumably it is in these terms that he thinks he is least inadequately expressed for most people throughout most of history. The existential-ontological language is not easy to understand; but the language of love, Fatherhood, free forgiveness and so on has communicated effectively for centuries, (and I believe that it still does). Of course some of the imagery will need changing, as anyone working in a different culture knows. Of course there is a need for what the Bible Societies in their new *Good News Bible* call 'dynamic equivalents'. But the sheer acceptabilof a service such as Series 3 Holy Communion, and the enormous sales of modern English Bibles are strong evidence of effective communication using the old beliefs and many of the old picture words. The credible alternative has yet to emerge, We may be pardoned for being sceptical as to whether it ever will.

3. THE USE OF BIBLICAL IMEGERY IN WORSHIP

by David L. Frost

Our medieval kings kept by them a Fool; whose obvious disabilities served to remind them of the limits placed on all human reason, and whose licensed gibes might (on occasions) cut down the pride of princes. He served also to recall that those for whom those princes made laws and dispensations more nearly resembled the condition of the fool than of the master; but chiefly there seems to have been a hope that the Fool's very derangement might mean at times that he had access to truths closed to more rational minds. It is some such role that I have proposed to myself to justify my presence over a number of years at the court of liturgy, and as an eavesdropper in the more august halls of theology.

But now the court of liturgy is under attack from its erstwhile ambassador from theology[1]; and since my betters have not yet taken up the challenge, it falls to me to tinkle my bells and put my bauble into an aggressive stance. And there is some appropriateness in giving the Fool the right of reply, for liturgy must chiefly be concerned not with the scruples and niceties of an intellectual elite but with the beliefs and emotions of Christian people at large.

The charge is that modern liturgy (and in particular, Series 3), with its insistent reference back to the Bible for idea and for image, ignores almost entirely the achievements of modern biblical scholarship and of the theology developed as a consequence of that scholarship.[2] It is complained that Series 3 in its expression of the Christian faith belongs more to the third century than to the twentieth; though, if I am right in asserting the necessarily popular basis of liturgy, the critics of Series 3 have already conceded that there is yet no case for change, for they see the biblicism of the liturgy as only one further instance of a regrettable tendency in clergy and laity alike to drag their feet at first sight of the deserts of modernism.

Yet from the Fool's end of the table, it is by no means clear that the bulk of Christians are wrong when, with a mixture of intuition and common-sense, they resist the pressures of the scholars. They have had suggested to them that aspects of Christian doctrine or of its biblical expression are a hindrance to evangelism; that the imagery by which the Bible conveys Christian truth is becoming obsolete; and again, that Christian doctrine itself, being fundamentally conditioned by its first century origins, needs radical alteration if it is to be accommodated to twentieth century thought. These three criticisms tend to be conflated and confused (perhaps for tactical reasons)[3]; but each is a distinct issue, and each is receiving some kind of answer in the Church at large.

[1] J. L. Houlden, 'Liturgy and her Companions' in *The Eucharist Today*, ed. R. C. D. Jasper (S.P.C.K., 1974), pp.168-76.
[2] Houlden's attack is taken up and developed in T. G. A. Baker, *Questioning Worship* (SCM, 1977).
[3] As in Maurice Wiles, *The Remaking of Christian Doctrine* (SCM, 1974).

On the issue of evangelism, it is increasingly apparent that old-style Christian rationalism is of interest chiefly to a small and ageing minority. Those who need miracles explained away are only a handful compared to those who run after Uri Geller, who read Professor John Taylor's investigations of him, who go to faith-healers, or who dabble in the occult. Astrology and witchcraft flourish, and belief in evil spirits seems no bar to achieving a following. The sciences themselves are much more willing to entertain notions of telepathy or of extra-sensory perception. With a new openness of mind in the public goes a new understanding of how reality may be talked about through image and metaphor: we are no longer the prisoners of literalism. And even doctrines of a Final Catastophe and a Second Coming, which have embarrassed us for so long, look increasingly acceptable in a situation where it seems each day more probable that we will destroy our world by nuclear conflict. For good and ill, the world of the twentieth century is much closer to that of the first century than many of our theologians are ready to admit: faced with the growth of exorcism, those fifty or so theologians who wrote to *The Times* did not ask for a commission of inquiry on which various disciplines might be represented but, in effect, begged the Archbishop to 'tell the nasty thing to go away'.

Of course, truth might compel us to change our attitudes, but expedience no longer does. The worldwide growth of the fundamentalist churches, especially the Pentecostals, suggests that biblical imagery has lost none of its power to communicate the Christian message. I will argue in a moment that that imagery has an archetypal validity which makes it irreplaceable; but that would be no reason to retain it if the doctrines it expressed had been shown to be a human creation rather than a divine revelation. Maurice Wiles and his associates[1] ground their theology on a total agnosticism about the life and words of Christ, an agnosticism derived from the supposed conclusions of New Testament criticism (though New Testament scholars are taken to task for not being as sceptical as they should be!). The ordinary Christian (and the liturgist) has therefore to look hard at the claims of New Testament scholarship.

Looked at from outside, biblical scholarship has all the characteristics of a necessarily inexact discipline, capable at best of limited verification. It may be less offensive if I describe the vices of my own discipline, which also handles literary texts. We suffer almost daily from defective methodology, circular argument, unexamined *a priori* assumptions, uncritical reliance on the work of others, hypotheses that become established fact in the course of argument, possibilities left unconsidered because of hidden presuppositions beyond what the evidence warrants, evidence partially treated, evidence misrepresented, evidence ignored. Our worst exponents often cherish a myth that we all share in a quasi-scientific enterprise, proceeding like natural scientists from hypothesis to experimentation, to verification, to further hypothesis. Our movement is more often crab-wise, from partial truth back into nonsense, to partial reply, then to rediscovery. Our faith is that we progress; but we do not proceed in orderly fashion, most of our conclusions are tentative, and our most cherished notions are liable to be overthrown.

[1] J Hick (ed.), *The Myth of God Incarnate* (SCM, 1977).

The literary man venturing into biblical studies finds some all too familiar symptoms. He has also the suspicion that on questions such as authorship-testing, problems such as the characteristics of 'oral tradition' or principles for fragmenting texts, the biblical scholar often lags behind developments in related disciples. The tale is cherished of how one Morton put St. Paul through a computer, and how an American professor subjected James Joyce to the same linguistic test: the computer concluded that *Ulysses* was written by seven authors, none of whom wrote *A Portrait of the Artist as a Young Man*.[1] John Robinson's recent book *Redating the New Testament* gave substance to many of the literary world's doubts about the dating methods used by New Testament scholars. I take it that Robinson intended primarily an exercise in scepticism, showing that as good if not better arguments could be adduced for putting the books of the New Testament *before* AD 70 rather than after. But Robinson's arguments affect every aspect of New Testament scholarship: for the supposed period of 'oral tradition' during which the young Church 'moulded' doctrine may have been shorter than we thought, and we perhaps have to consider the likeli-hood of ear- and eye-witnesses to the events of the early decades surviving at the time when most of the texts were composed.

The difficulty for literary critics and for biblical scholars is that the public knows the texts from which we work—our limitations can be only too apparent. T. G. A. Baker[2], criticising the Series 3 treatment of the Ascension, asserts that 'it is generally agreed among New Testament scholars that the idea of a temporary restoration of the Risen Lord to quasi-physical conditions, followed by the ascension as a second and separable act, is to be found only in Luke-Acts'—the general reader knows that the same notion is implied in John 20.27, 20.17. Again, Maurice Wiles writes that 'Talk of (Christ's) pre-existence ought probably in most, perhaps all, cases to be understood . . . to indicate the divine purpose being achieved through him, rather than pre-existence of a fully personal kind.'[3] The ordinary reader recalls the obvious implications of Luke 10.18, Mark 12.35-37, Philippians 2.5-7, 2 Corinthians 8.9. Wiles' references to two articles on the subject hardly compensate for his neglect of the evidence: you cannot make gaffs like these and command the respect of the public. Liturgists, though they are rarely fundamentalists or unconcerned with the questions that New Testament scholarship proposes, find that they have to take account of a widespread scepticism about the practices of New Testament scholarship. Very few of its conclusions are so unassailable or so universally accepted that we can make use of them. And while New Testament scholarship contains such figures as C. F. D. Moule and theology such men as Karl Barth and his followers (all of them attracting the contemptuous label of 'conservative'), it cannot be argued that modern scholarship speaks with a united voice that we ignore at our peril.

The attack on Biblical imagery was in part a prelude and a cover to an assault on Biblical doctrine: this is hardly surprising, for the *way* something is said is not readily distinguishable from *what* is said. The point can be

---

1 See S. Schoenbaum, *Internal Evidence and Elizabethan Dramatic Authorship* (1966), passim.
2 Baker, *Questioning Worship*, p.46.
3 Wiles, *Remaking of Christian Doctrine*, p.53.

illustrated from John Robinson's early attempts[1] to substitute for the metaphors of God 'out there' or 'up there' an image of an immanent God, *panentheistic,* the 'ground of our being'. This seemed to rescue us from an outdated cosmology and to bring us into line with the God of the mystics, the 'God within'. But the traditional Christian imagery had emphasized the distinction between God and his creation, and it presented our initial experience as one of *separation* from God, requiring a divine initiative from *outside* man's sphere to repair the breach. The 'new' imagery presented God not as someone who comes looking for us, but as someone we might discover by an act of will, by contemplation or self-contemplation, by a decision to go 'exploring into God'. Its implications were Pelagian. Moreover, 'Panentheism' tended to blur the traditional distinction between good and evil, for it presented the divine will as equally fulfilled in all creation. Robinson found himself writing that 'God is *in* the cancer as he is in the sunset . . . Both are among the faces of God, the one terrible, the other beautiful'.[2] In trying to avoid the images of conflict, images of Light versus Darkness, the modified dualism of the New Testament, Robinson spoke of a 'supra-personal God', 'beyond Good and Evil'; thereby denying the full seriousness of evil, whilst maintaining insistently that he was not doing so. John Hick's more sophisticated *Evil and the God of Love* ended in much the same contradiction.

In the same way, it is doctrinal objections which lie behind Houlden's and Baker's attacks on the imagery by which Series 3 expresses Creation and Redemption. There is nothing offensive to modern science in the metaphor of the 'acts of God', for Series 3 speaks of a God who 'created all things *from the beginning'* and who is therefore the author, designer and director of evolutionary processes and of the daily creation of life: Series 3 asserts final causes, an area beyond the field of natural science. (In passing, we may note that Series 3, while not denying the fact of universal sinfulness, is not committed to a literal understanding of the Genesis story of the Fall). Where the shoe pinches is over the doctrine of the Incarnation, for Series 3 describes that as a mighty act of God, a metaphor which T. G. A. Baker would brand as 'interventionist'. But you either believe that God was in Christ in a way *radically different* to the way in which God was in, say, William Shakespeare—or you do not. If you do believe in a radical difference, you will find 'interventionist' imagery unavoidable. In fact, Baker (p.48) indicates his involvement in 'the problem presented today by the traditional doctrine of the uniqueness and finality of Christ', and Houlden has now declared his hand.

Doctrinal preoccupations can easily warp one's judgment of the effectiveness of Biblical images. Houlden, for example[3], criticises Series 3 when it praises God 'for creation through Jesus, his living Word': he complains that 'We appeal thereby to a biblical and patristic concept, that of Christ as the pre-existent Logos, which is more remote from present-day thought than almost any other and which is so far removed from readily accessible

---

[1] J. A. T. Robinson, *Honest to God* (SCM, 1963), further pursued in *Exploration into God* (SCM, 1967).
[2] Robinson, *Exploration into God,* p.109.
[3] Houlden in *The Eucharist Today,* p.173.

imagery that its evocative power is minimal, except for the initatied.' In fact, the image of 'the Word' is archetypal, and has no necessary connection with first century understanding of the 'Logos'. By words men communicate their will and make their inner intentions operative. Moreover, psychologists of cognition such as the late Sir Frederick Bartlett[1] have shown us how the young child relies on language to categorize and bring order to the multitude of sense stimuli which assault him. The mother holds up an object, pronounces a word—and 'saucer' is established as a 'schema' for round, white objects. The child explores the object, and 'saucer' is discovered to be hard and smooth; it is held edge-on, and seen to offer on occasions the appearance of being thin and white, pointed at either end. Later, its size and shape will be distinguished from a similar object called a 'plate'. The 'word' (probably a sound/object compound to the child) is vital in this process: it is a tool in establishing contact with one's environment, in making sense of it—and later it will become a 'word of power', helping the child to express its wishes and gain control over its world, by speech and by writing. You have to be very scholastic to assert that 'Christ the living Word' is an outdated metaphor.

So it is with many Biblical images: they have a psychological force derived from our earliest childhood experiences. The metaphors of Light and Darkness I have already mentioned. But other metaphors which seem more obviously superseded may also have an archetypal validity. I once argued that the declining power of twentieth century monarchs made metaphors of the Kingship of God less meaningful[2]—I now doubt if I was right. For Jung has identified the Father/King image as an archetype, probably connected with the child's early apprehension of the (to him) unlimited power of the first human beings of which he is conscious. 'The figures of both father and king tend to retain within those deeper levels of the mind to which poetry may penetrate something of the *mana* that invested the first representative of a power akin to, but vastly beyond, that of the individual emerging into self-consciousness'[3]. It is well-known that Freud saw images of God as being extrapolations from the child's experience of his father: it is also now well understood that God and the parent are so linked in the human mind that a defective relationship with the parent may prove an almost insurmountable barrier to any experience of a loving 'Heavenly Father'. I doubt if a diminution in the power of contemporary monarchs much affects the reverberation of images of kingship and fatherhood at these deep levels of the mind: certainly, a brief check on my son's story-books hardly suggests any decline in the imaginative appeal of the image of the all-powerful king.

What I am arguing for is more thought and more humility, before Biblical images are recklessly discarded. It may be that Jewish sacrificial practices are not widely understood, and that doctrines of the atonement as sacrifice are not wholly satisfactory. But before we censor images of sacrifice out of

1 F. C. Bartlett, in his classic *Remembering* (CUP, 1932) and elsewhere.
2 D. L. Frost, *The Language of Series 3* (Grove Booklet on Ministry and Worship No. 12, 1973), p.14.
3 Maud Bodkin, *Archetypal Patterns in Poetry* (O.U.P., 1934), p.17.

our liturgy we must remember the needs of the guilt-ridden, the pathetic rituals of placation and subsittionary sacrifice that any psychiatrist will describe as endemic among his patients—Christianity has traditionally offered us a placatory sacrifice that *worked*. Again, we need to be more knowledgeable about what modern studies such as psychology and anthropology are *really* saying. Baker (p.27) voices an often-heard request that in talk of 'eating Christ's body and blood' we avoid 'highly offensive notions of cannibalism'. We now know that a major motive in the practice of cannibalism is to acquire the powers and characteristics of the person you eat—it may not be a 'nice' image for communion, but it cannot be denied that it is a precise metaphor for what we are after!

More thought and more humility—for what runs through our modern discussions of theology and of New Testament scholarship is a recurrent note of *superbia intellectualis,* of intellectual pride. The Fool is not just being obscurantist or intellectually lazy when he asks that scholars bring to their own mental constructs the same scepticism that they bring to biblical texts. Christianity has always been 'to the Greeks foolishness', and in its pages the fools have the better record: for the God of Christianity 'brings to nothing the wisdom of the wise'.

4. THE ROLE OF THE LECTIONARY

by John Tiller

A pause for breath in the endless chanting? A chance for the choir to find their places for the next musical offering? An opportunity for some member of the laity to play a part in the service? Or for the drama group to go to town? A preview of the preacher's text? Paying homage to Holy Writ? These are some of the roles that the Bible reading appears to play in the worship of different congregations. When looked at closely, none of them is valid enough to give this activity the unquestioned place it has in almost all church services. Occasionally of late a voice has been heard suggesting that extensive public reading of the Scriptures is only justified in circumstances of widespread illiteracy. The trend in liturgical revision, however, has been in the reverse direction. Pauses for reverent meditation upon what has been read; and the introduction of congregational responses to the affirmation 'This is the Word of the Lord' at the end of the readings, now serve to underline the solemnity of the performance. Rather than discussing why the Bible should be read in worship, debate focusses on the relative merits of different schemes for organising the biblical material into a usable lectionary. A satisfactory solution to this problem, however, may depend upon an agreed understanding of the purpose of the exercise. The object of this chapter is to suggest three specific functions which combine to give the lectionary its authentic role.

The first function *links the congregation to the Christian tradition.* It is true that for many today the activity of worship is distinctly over-burdened with the 'dead weight' of tradition. A dull routine of mental, verbal and physical exercises devoid of the liberating breath of the Spirit is blamed for the sheer boredom that prevails in many churches on Sundays. Yet supposing for a moment that a completely spontaneous, charismatic style of worship quite unaffected by previous practice were possible (in fact it is not!), then the occasion would have the nature of a purely random event, following from nothing and leading to nothing. In that situation the Jesus of history and the Christ of faith would have no necessary relationship. Today's worship is in fact linked to that of the Christian Church through time and space by means of the common tradition about Jesus. It seems likely that the origin of the written Gospels lies in the liturgical need for this tradition to be preserved. Other links with the tradition are of course in existence: the creeds (cf. 1 Cor. 15.3); the Lord's Supper (1 Cor. 11.23); and the developed liturgies, which in their infancy expressed a concern for 'orthodoxy' in worship (cf. Hippolytus, *Apostolic Tradition,* 9); not to mention the Christian festivals. The last two of these are, however, subsidiary links; and the creed is a minimum statement of the tradition, which is hardly adequate as a resource for all Christian worship. Even the Lord's Supper may not be regarded as an independent link in the opinion of those who, like the present writer, consider that the eucharistic action is identified by the use of the scriptural words of institution.[1]

The reading of the Scriptures, then, gives catholicity to worship, and it does so because it is by this means above all other that Christians are

---

[1] For a contrary view see J. A. Baker, in *Thinking about the Eucharist,* ed. I. T. Ramsey (SCM, 1972), pp.38-58.

united to their common tradition. The additional use of other non-biblical readings in worship may be appropriate on particular occasions, but these can never in principle provide an alternative to the Scripture lessons, which alone are able to play this determinative role. As the historic eucharistic lectionary reveals, the Gospels are the core of the tradition, but the Epistles and the Old Testament lessons relate the figure of Jesus to the purpose of God and the life of the Church. When on Sundays the early Christians read together the records of the apostles and writings of the prophets for 'as long as time allowed', they stood in conscious relationship to the synagogue practice of reading from the law and the prophets.[1] The restoration in recent years of Old Testament readings at the Eucharist has been an important step in strengthening a sense of being linked to the age-old purpose of God to sum up all things in Christ.

Need such dependence upon tradition be a dead thing? Not if there is any sense of the inspiration of the Scriptures! They link us not to a dead teacher, but to the living Christ, through whom the purpose of God is still being worked out in the world.[2]

The second function of the lectionary is *to impose upon the worshippers the duty of listening.*

> 'God, the Lord God, has spoken
> and summoned the world from the rising to the setting sun.
> God shines out from Zion, perfect in beauty.
> Our God is coming and will not keep silence . . .
> Listen, my people, and I will speak;
> I will bear witness against you, O Israel:
> I am God, your God,
> shall I not find fault with your sacrifices,
> though your offerings are before me always? . . .
> God's word to the wicked man is this:
> What right have you to recite my laws
> and make so free with the words of my covenant,
> you who hate correction
> and turn your back when I am speaking?'   *(Psalm 50)*

Here is a classic description of vain worship which is too busy to stop and listen to what God is saying. There is nothing to be gained from occupying ourselves in prayers, music and offerings if they divert attention from the fundamental concern that God is addressing us, and, as the Venite puts it, 'You shall know his power today if you will listen to his voice.' (Ps. 95.7).

Undoubtedly the Word of God may break through in unpredictable ways and in unexpected parts of worship. It would be foolish to limit God's part to the readings and (if all goes well) the sermon. It is also true, as the quotation from Psalm 50 presupposes, that it was possible to recite the Torah quite happily without actually hearing what God was saying. This same heedless, unprofitable reading of the Bible is also possible in Christian worship. But the formal space created by the lectionary makes the point that the 'better part' of our service is, like Mary's, to sit at Jesus' feet and listen to his words (Luke 10.39).

[1] Justin, *First Apology*, 67.3. See further J. A. Lamb, 'The place of the Bible in the Liturgy', in *The Cambridge History of the Bible*, vol. i, ed. P. R. Ackroyd and C. F. Evans, (Cambridge, 1970), pp.563-86.
[2] This is well illustrated, in, for example, 2 Peter 3.9, 15f.

The implications of this for the lectionary need careful consideration. For one thing, any acceptable scheme needs to be sufficiently comprehensive. This is not to say that every chapter of the Bible is suitable material for public reading in worship. But unless the readings are representative of the whole range of biblical literature and include all the major themes, congenial or not, we may literally be gagging the Word of God. The more restricted the amount of Scripture used, the greater will be the danger of subjective selection and thus of human censorship. It is questionable, for example, whether the Series 3 eucharistic lectionary of the Church of England is justified in omitting parts of so basic a portion of Scripture as the Sermon on the Mount. It is indeed questionable whether anything in the Gospels should be omitted from the Sunday services of the local church. So can a two-year cycle of readings hope to be satisfactory as a selection?[1]

The other criterion for lectionary provision which arises from the need to listen, fully and seriously, to what the Bible actually says, is to be seen in the choice of how to divide up the material. Because of accustomed habits over the length of readings, and on the whole an unadventurous approach to the question of how to present a passage within the context of worship, most devisers of lectionary schemes try to make the Scripture text fit a predetermined ideal length. It is strictly irrelevant to discuss what the average length of a reading should be. Natural units of the Bible should be read as a whole. This does not necessitate a solid block of reading at one point in the service. Longer units can be treated by alternate listening and response as the narrative is read section by section through a service. The lesson is not 'a word in edgeways': the liturgy arises from a listening congregation. And continuous reading is needed on Sundays . . .

The third function of the lectionary is *to enable the liturgy to become the vehicle of proclamation.* The Church is called to hear the Word of God. But it is not expected to remain silent. The Psalter focusses this call:

> 'I will praise thee, O Lord, with all my heart,
> I will tell the story of thy marvellous acts.'

And: 'O God, we re-enact the story of thy true love within thy temple;
the praise thy name deserves, O God, is heard at earth's farthest bounds'[2]

Christians are specifically summoned, as a royal priesthood, to proclaim the saving power of God in Christ (1 Pet. 2.9; 1 Cor. 11.26). This is the theme of their worship, and of course the whole liturgy, seen from one aspect, is a proclamation. But the Bible and the liturgy stand in the relation of testimony and praise. Without the readings the biblical allusions in the hymns and prayers would be lost. It would be like joining a cheering crowd without having heard what the proclamation was about.

Something similar to this happens when a lectionary is formally in use, but the hymns and prayers bear no relation to its content. A lectionary makes demands upon the rest of the service by way of response, reaction, development, appropriation. When this takes place the liturgy takes on the character of a proclamation of God's Word for that occasion, place and people. The question is not whether a Bible reading is appropriate for a particular service; but what appropriate service arises from a particular reading.

---

[1] For alternatives see my article 'Towards a better Lectionary: The effective liturgical use of the Gospels', in *The Churchman,* vol. 87, 1973, pp.182-189; and C. Hart, 'A Lectionary of Biblically Controlled Service', in vol. 91, 1977, pp.134-145.
[2] Ps. 9.1; 48.9f; (cf.52.9; 89.1; 96.1-3; 105.1f; 106.2; etc.).

5. THE ROLE OF THE SERMON
by Ian D. Bunting

Imagine a bridge spanning a deep gorge. On one side stands God and, on the other, contemporary Man. They look across at each other above the abyss which some call, 'sin and rebellion' and others, 'alienation and estrangement'. The bridge is known after its builder, Jesus Christ. The purpose of the architect is that Man may pass safely to God. But is the bridge safe? Does it actually reach the other side? Man is very conscious of the danger which lies at the bottom. Yet standing upon the bridge is one who beckons to him to cross over. He is the preacher. His task is to summon, challenge and encourage us to step out in faith.

The illustration is simple. In reality, as we sit in our pews, we find it hard to stir ourselves. The questions of our day drive home. Is not the preacher a man like us? We have learnt to suspect the propagandist as he tries to persuade us to change our ways with words which sound like institutionally protected platitudes. Harvey Cox retells one of Kierkegaard's parables about a travelling circus which burst into flames outside a Danish village. The clown, already dressed for his performance, was despatched to get help from the local inhabitants before the fire engulfed their houses. In the market place the painted clown called desperately for help to extinguish the flames. The more he appealed to them, the more the villagers laughed at this novel way of gathering an audience . . . until the fire spread across the fields and their homes were destroyed around them.[1] Thus, in the ears of the hearer, can the Word be compromised. The preacher, because of the church in which he preaches, or the context in which he performs, may be as incredible as the clown. And, in the strictest sense, if he *is* incredible, then the results are as catastrophic. He has a life-saving function to fulfil.

A second question relates to the message he brings. In a perceptive comment on modern preaching, C. H. Dodd compared the sermon technique of today, which chooses texts to fit themes, with the pattern of preaching in the New Testament.

> 'To select from the New Testament certain passages which seem to have a modern ring and to declare that these represent the permanent element in it is not necessarily to preach the Gospel. It is moreover easy to be mistaken, on a superficial reading, about the true meaning of passages which strike us as congenial'.[2]

The vast majority of preachers today offer topical sermons. That is, they begin from some situation deemed to be relevant and proceed to illustrate their theme, or to support it, by means of appropriately selected texts. This practice leaves the thoughtful hearer with a deep uncertainty. Is the Bible meant to be a compendium of proof text and illustrative stories? Is not the preacher in danger of missing the deep truths which underlie the passages he employs and, if he does that, what authority, other than his own interpretation, has he got for using the Bible in this way? The bridge may never actually reach the other side.

[1] Harvey Cox, *The Secular City* (SCM, London, 1965), p.247.
[2] C. H. Dodd, *The Apostolic Preaching and Its Developments,* (Hodder and Stoughton, London, 1936), p.93 (1972 edition).

A third question confronts the hearer in his pew as he wonders whether the preacher's communication is reliable. Is the language he uses a useful or even a safe guide to find God today? Writing of the way he believes the biblical images have been misused in modern liturgy, J. L. Houlden complains,

> 'There has been little sign of any serious attempt to consider whether these words and images still carry their former vividness or are intelligible expressions of what is to be said'.[1]

It is a complaint many will also want to level against the sermon in church. Even if biblical language and imagery can be understood by the people, how far is the understanding the same as that of our fathers who first heard the message and passed it on? The preacher who stands boldly upon the biblical pillar which supports the bridge finds it hard to persuade 20th century Man that there is not a gaping hole between them.

It will already be apparent that the preacher has awesome responsibility as he tries to help men and women, to come to God. At whatever point upon the bridge he stands he is vulnerable and exposed to the chill winds of current scepticism and uncertainty. If he stands solely at one end, close to the scandalous particularities of God's self-revelation, he is beyond hailing distance from his hearers burdened with the relativities and plurality of 20th century thought. If, on the other hand, he stands solely at the near end of the bridge he lacks both the right location and the authoritative summons which can actually be heard as a challenge and a spur to cross over. The preacher will therefore have to be self-aware in relation to God and the Gospel and sensitive to his hearers and the way they are receiving the message he brings. Then he must be able to move with some confidence to and fro across the bridge calling now from this point and now from that so that he may be heard as the messenger of God he is sent to be.

The preacher's first responsibility will be to stand firmly upon the pillar of God's self-revelation. Karl Barth writes in the Preface to the first edition of *Romans;*

> 'The critical historical method of Biblical research has its validity. It points to the preparation for understanding that is never superfluous. But if I had to choose between it and the old doctrine of inspiration, I would decidedly lay hold of the latter. It has the greater, deeper, more important validity, for it points to the actual work of understanding, without which all preparation is useless. I am happy not to have to choose between the two. But my whole intention was directed to looking through the historical to the spirit of the Bible, which is the eternal Spirit. What was once serious is still serious today, and what today is serious, and not just accidental and peripheral, stands in direct relation to what was once serious. Our questions, if we understand ourselves aright, are the questions of Paul, and Paul's answers, if their light illuminates us, must be our answers'.[2]

1 Ed. R. C. D. Jasper, *The Eucharist Today* (S.P.C.K. London, 1974) p.173.
2 Ed. James M. Robinson and John R. Cobb, *New Frontiers in Theology,* vol. II, *The New Hermeneutic* (Harper & Row, New York, 1964) p.22. (translated from the original German).

Karl Barth represents the resounding 'No' to modern self-confident Man. We cannot, by our searching, find God and therefore the preacher who aims to help others must himself stand upon the gracious self-revelation of God in Christ. The Bible is the supreme and only truly authoritative witness to that revelation. What God has revealed in creation or in natural law or even in the Old Testament scriptures is not salvific apart from Christ. Man can manufacture no bridges for himself even with God's aid. The bridge is constructed from God's side and the Scriptures undergird the span. The preacher will then, first and foremost, be an expositor of the Bible. Does that mean that every sermon will have a text? That it is possible to proclaim the living Word of God without direct quotation of biblical texts would seem to be true from the Old and New Testament prophets and from Jesus' own teaching method as well as our own experience of hearing, for example, various parabolic presentations of Christian truth, but normally we abandon the Bible and demythologize its imagery at our peril; but more of that later. The preacher who cannot bring a Word from God based upon a straight and honest interpretation of the Scriptures deserves the lack of confidence he creates in his congregation. They may like him as a friend. They may admire him as a seeker like themselves. They may even follow him as one who has stepped out further in faith than they have themselves. But there will be no salvation if the word preached is not God's Word.

For Anglicans, the Word has always been closely associated with the faithful reading and exposition of the Scriptures. Some would say that this association, which is rooted in the Reformation and the Elizabethan settlement, has been too close and has given rise to the bibliolatry which observers feel is deep-rooted in English Christianity. Be that as it may, there is no doubt that Richard Hooker was not just speaking for himself when he wrote, 'we therefore have no word of God but the Scripture'.[1] This traditional Anglican stance was maintained against the Puritans who held that preaching was the normally effective means to salvation. Thomas Cartwright, for instance, likens preaching to a 'lifting or heaving up of our Saviour Christ', more effectual than bare reading of the Scriptures.[2] Anglicans have resisted this subtle temptation to carry the word preached higher than Bible itself. The reading of the Scriptures and their exposition lie at the heart of Anglican liturgy and the same is still true today even if, in most churches of all traditions, the minister is preoccupied with the peculiar problems of trying to interpret the Bible in a way which has meaning to those who listen.

One wonders sometimes if the preacher today is not too pre-occupied with the question of relevance. He must, after all, let God be God and allow the Holy Spirit to do what he certainly cannot do himself, namely to bring conviction, conversion and sanctification. Indeed it may be argued that the most dated, useless and arid of all liturgies are those which have sold out to the current idol of relevance. It is fascinating, for example, to pick up an

[1] Richard Hooker, *Of the Laws of Ecclesiastical Polity*, Book 5 (Everyman's Library Vol. 2, J. M. Dent, London, 1907) p.77.
[2] *op. cit.* p.93n.

American liturgy of 1971, *A Liberation Prayer Book*.[1] It is an Episcopalian (i.e. Anglican) compilation produced in the wake of the political and social upheavals of the late 1960s for the Free Church of Berkeley, California. The traditional liturgy is demythologized and cast into the language of revolution and cultural immediacy. The imagery is taken over from the jungle of a twentieth century industrial and consumer-oriented life-style. Within seven years the whole book is unusable, and even laughable, in its irrelevance and archaic world-view. We let go of our biblical roots at our peril and we wed the spirit of our age only to be widowed in the next. The answer is not to abandon the biblical imagery in order to rid ourselves of obsolete stories. The symbols and stories of the Bible which lie at the heart of Christian faith cannot be destroyed or even superseded by empirical criticism and invention. They actually participate in the reality of what they represent. The preacher's task is to enable them to touch men with their ancient power. Undoubtedly preachers in our age have lost confidence in this particular vocation. Hence they have tended to *use* the Bible to serve their immediate purposes. The Bible has lost its intrinsic property as the supremely authoritative witness to God's activity in the world and the ground of Christian proclamation. Instead preachers have fallen into the trap of ascribing to their own or the churches' perspectives a wholly unjustified status which is a very horrid form of modern idolatry.

Anglicans have traditionally believed, in the words of Article XIX, that, 'The visible Church of Christ is a congregation of faithful men, in which the pure Word of God is preached . . .'. The words and pictures of the Bible are not just models which can be discarded as only loosely related to the Truth. Nor, incidentally, are they rigid and wooden forms of propositional truth which we can simply systematize and serve up for all time. John Robinson wrote in 1620;

> 'I am verily persuaded the Lord hath more truth yet to break forth out of his holy word. For my part I cannot sufficiently bewail the condition of those reformed churches which are come to a period in religion and will go at present no farther than the instruments of their reformation. The Lutherans cannot be drawn to go beyond what Luther saw; whatever part of his will God has revealed to John Calvin, they will rather die than embrace it; and the Calvinists, you see, stick fast where they were left by that great man of God who yet saw not all things . . .'.

The preacher stands under the Word of God recorded in the Scriptures and committed to let God speak, confident that the Bible and its imagery is still capable, by God's Spirit, of being the source of Christian life and hope.

So far we have tried to underline the importance of starting from a biblical foundation if the message which the preacher brings is to be credibly related to the origin and source of our faith in the person of Jesus Christ. A too-ready submission to the canons of relevance will betray the hearer who has come to receive a word from God. But how is the preacher to carry the word home to his listeners?

This has been attempted in various ways since the Reformation. John Calvin, for example, preached what was, in effect, a commentary upon the

---

1 The Free Church of Berkeley, *The Covenant of Peace, A Liberation Prayer Book* (Morehouse-Barlow, New York, 1971).

biblical text. His sermons were therefore based upon a *lectio continua,* a regular and consecutive reading of the Scriptures. First he exegeted the passage, then he expounded its meaning, then he applied it to his congregation and he ended with an exhortation to faith and obedience. An English preacher who followed much in this tradition was Matthew Henry.

'The Word of God is designed to be not only a light to our eyes, the entertaining subject of our contemplation, but a light to our feet and a lamp to our path . . . we must therefore, in searching the Scriptures, inquire, not only, What is this? but What is this to us? What use may we make of it? How may we accommodate it to some of the purposes of that Divine and heavenly life which, by the grace of God, we are resolved to live? Inquiries of this kind I have . . . aimed to answer.'[1]

As a method this has much to commend it. The text of the sermon selects itself, for the preacher works through the Scriptures. The commentary method ensures, so far as possible, a proper survey of the biblical material. The preacher is less able to adulterate the pure Word of God. The commitment to application forbids him from simply escaping into the pastness of the received tradition. But all this does presuppose a certain understanding of how God speaks and may establish the independence of that Word at the expense of its living impact upon a twentieth century congregation not so well equipped as our fathers to understand and apply what the Bible says to their own situation.

The most interesting developments in the twentieth century come from the Lutheran stable. In the Reformation period Luther believed that Christ ought to be preached,

'to the end that faith in him may be established, that he may not only be Christ, but be Christ for thee and for me, and that what is said of him and what his name denotes may be effectual in us.'[2]

A clear modern exponent of this understanding is Gerhard Ebeling. Verbal communication is not simply the imparting of knowledge but an event which actually changes the situation. It is actually possible to enter into the meaning of the message preached. We can enter into the experience of the truth which is being described or explained. We can meet with the living Christ, and be changed by him, in the same way as the disciples were changed. The preacher thus becomes the agent of an authentic encounter with the person of Christ.

'The content of the word and the fulfilling of the word, its reaching its goal, are identical. A word of this kind does what it says, it fulfils what it promises. When faith and God are put together, we may put it thus: we are not concerned just with a piece of information about God, but with participation in him, that is, with an event in which God himself is communicated.'[3]

Although the reformers were certainly concerned to communicate the gospel simply, it is undoubtedly true to say that the emphasis has shifted, in

---

[1] Matthew Henry, *An Exposition of the Old and New Testaments,* (Partridge and Oakey, London, 1847) p.iii.
[2] *Works of Martin Luther* (six volumes, United Lutheran Publication House, Philadelphia, 1915-1932), vol. 2, pp.326f.
[3] Gerhard Ebeling, *The Nature of Faith* (Collins, Glasgow, 1961), p.87.

our day, from the messenger to the receiver, from what is said to what is heard. In an age when old world views and traditional religious languages have lost their currency this is healthy. After all, the teaching of Jesus himself had to make ground in the face of well-rooted tradition and prejudice expressed in the words and thought-forms of a culture alien to the Gospel. He did it by a hermeneutic which was novel for his day, through parables, unlike other contemporary parables, through demands which outraged the old interpreters of the law, and through seemingly irrational self-understandings. His purpose was that his hearers should enter into a life-transforming encounter with the living God. Ours should be too.

This means that the contemporary question cannot be ignored. Few preachers today will consciously do that but they may, usually through pressure of work, ask the question with insufficient rigour. Certainly critics of the pulpit frequently complain of both ill-informed comments on current affairs and trivial prescriptions for the deep-seated ills of our world. There is a right selectivity as the preacher chooses the particular Scriptures which he will expound. It will not be the artificial selectivity of liturgy-makers who impose themes upon, for example, the Sunday readings. Nor will it be the selectivity of the preacher who searches for clever or apposite texts. The Church has the responsibility for presenting a full-orbed gospel which meets us at whatever point we stand. Through the centuries she has done this by fastening upon a Word for the day. In the 16th century, for instance, it was 'Justification', today it is 'The King and the Kingdom'. There is, of course, the danger of falling into a form of cultural Christianity whereby the Word is forced into some current mode of thought. There is the further danger that the understanding of a former age will be fossilized and become the millstone around the necks of succeeding generations. But if the Spirit still guides the Church then we may believe that he will lead the preacher in his exposition of the Truth as it is in Jesus Christ.

In this essay we have tried to establish the exposition of the Scriptures as the essential foundation of preaching. We have gone on to agree that a certain selectivity in the choice of Scriptures to be used is necessary if we are to preach the Word for today. How in practice are we to go about our preaching programme on the basis of these two cardinal principles? One helpful, but fairly traditional, answer is suggested by Leonard Griffith who patterns his pulpit ministry upon the Bible, the Liturgical Calendar and the Doctrine of the Trinity.

> 'From September to Advent the theme is God the Father and is usually based on a specific area of the Old Testament. From Christmas to Easter the sermons derive from the Gospels and attempt to set forth God the Son. From Pentecost to the summer I preach from the Acts or the Epistles about God the Holy Spirit.'[1]

Allowing room for Festivals and topical series, as he does, this seems to mark out useful boundaries for the preacher's selectivity. Within those boundaries I would want to preach short series of expository sermons which follow consecutively through a section or book of the Bible. It is well attested moreover that congregations respond warmly to biblical exposition which informs them of the facts of their faith, which instructs them in the implications of it and which enables an encounter with the Christ who is the same yesterday, today and for ever. Thus men and women come safely across the bridge to God.

[1] Leonard Griffiths, *The Need to Preach* (Hodder and Stoughton, London, 1971), p.23.

USING THE BIBLE IN WORSHIP

Biblical language in the prayers and other liturgical texts in use in the Churches has come under some steady attack in recent years. This Liturgical Study is a trenchant restatement of the case for biblical language in these contexts, along with a further consideration of the positive role which the Bible itself has to play in worship in both lectionary readings and preaching. Scholars, liturgists and pastors combine together to issue a strong counter-challenge to some critics of, for example, the thought-forms of Series 3 Communion.

THE COVER ILLUSTRATION
. . . is by Alex Grenfell.

GROVE LITURGICAL STUDIES

This series of weighty studies appears quarterly, replacing in each third month the slighter 'Grove Booklets on Ministry and Worship'. Price **75p.**

1 **SACRAMENTAL INITIATION COMPLETE IN BAPTISM**
by E. C. Whitaker
2 **LANGUAGE LITURGY AND MEANING** by A. C. Thiselton
3 **SHRINES FOR THE SAINTS: How Parish Churches Evolved**
4 **CENTRES FOR THE SERVANTS: Parish Plant Updated**
Both by Kenneth White
5 **ANAMNESIS IN THE EUCHARIST** by David Gregg
6 **THE LITURGY AND MUSIC: A Study of the Use of the Hymn in Two Liturgical Traditions**
by Robin A. Leaver
7 **WHAT DID CRANMER THINK HE WAS DOING?**
by Colin Buchanan
8 **HIPPOLYTUS: A text for students with translation, notes and commentary** by Geoffrey J. Cuming
9 **LAY PRESIDENCY AT THE EUCHARIST?**
Edited by Trevor Lloyd
10 **GREGORY DIX—TWENTY-FIVE YEARS ON**
by Kenneth Stevenson
11 **USING THE BIBLE IN WORSHIP**
Edited by Christopher Byworth
12 **WORSHIP IN THE NEW TESTAMENT**—(i) (December 1977)
13 **WORSHIP IN THE NEW TESTAMENT**—(ii) (March 1978)
by C. F. D. Moule (Reprinted from the standard textbook of this title previously published by Lutterworth Press)

For details of other Grove Books publications send for catalogue

ISSN 0306 0608   **ISBN** 0 905422 21 X

GROVE BOOKS
BRAMCOTE NOTTS. (0602-251114)

ınted by Hassall & Lucking Ltd., Cross Street, Long Eaton, Nottingham, NG10 1HD   Tel. L.E. 3292